A Day in the Life: Polar Animals

Polar Bear

Katie Marsico

www.raintreepublishers.co.uk
Visit our website to find out more information about Raintree books.

To order:
☎ Phone 0845 6044371
🖷 Fax +44 (0) 1865 312263
🖳 Email myorders@raintreepublishers.co.uk

Customers from outside the UK please telephone +44 1865 312262

Raintree is an imprint of Capstone Global Library Limited, a company incorporated in England and Wales having its registered office at 7 Pilgrim Street, London, EC4V 6LB – Registered company number: 6695582

Edited by Daniel Nunn, Rebecca Rissman, and Sian Smith
Designed by Joanna Hinton-Malivoire
Picture research by Hannah Taylor
Original illustrations © Capstone Global Library
Production by Victoria Fitzgerald
Originated by Capstone Global Library Ltd
Printed and bound in China by South China Printing Company Ltd

ISBN 978 1 406 22881 6 (hardback)
15 14 13 12 11
10 9 8 7 6 5 4 3 2 1

British Library Cataloguing in Publication Data
Marsico, Katie, 1980-
  Polar bear. -- (A day in the life. Polar animals)
  1. Polar bear--Juvenile literature.
  I. Title II. Series
  599.7'86-dc22

Acknowledgements
We would like to thank the following for permission to reproduce photographs: Alamy Images p. 21 (© Stuart Yates); Corbis pp. 4, 23c (Richard Berry/Design Pics), 14 (Chris Rainier); FLPA p. 7 (Minden Pictures/Flip Nicklin); Getty Images p. 6 (Daniel J. Cox); Photolibrary pp. 5 (Oxford Scientific/ Roland Mayr), 15 (Oxford Scientific/ Eric LeFranc), 17 (imagebroker/ Jorn Friedrich), 18 (Imagebroker RF), 20 (Picture Press/Thorsten Milse); Shutterstock pp. 8 (© Witold Kaszkin), 9, 23b (© Andy Farrer), 10 (© Lilyana Vynogradova), 11, 23a (© Nik Niklz), 12 (©Gentoo Multimedia Ltd.), 13, 23g (© Keith Levit), 16 (© Witold Kaszkin), 19, 23d (© littlesam), 22 (© Witold Kaszkin), 23f (© Danicek).

Cover photograph of a polar bear (Ursus maritimus) in Spitsbergen, Svalbard, Norway reproduced with permission of Photolibrary (age fotostock/ Morales Morales). Back cover photographs reproduced with permission of Shutterstock: nose (© Witold Kaszkin), snow pit (© littlesam).

The publisher would like to thank Michael Bright for his assistance in the preparation of this book.

Every effort has been made to contact copyright holders of material reproduced in this book. Any omissions will be rectified in subsequent printings if notice is given to the publisher.

Contents

Some words are shown in bold, **like this**.
You can find them in the glossary on page 23.

What is a polar bear?

Polar bears are large **mammals** that live near snow and ice.

Mammals have hair and feed their babies milk.

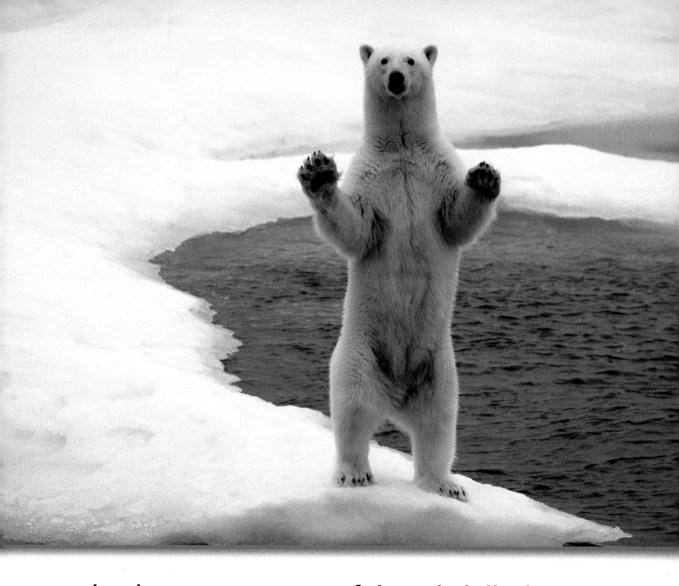

Polar bears are powerful and skilled hunters.

They are **predators** in many **polar** areas.

What do polar bears look like?

Polar bears are some of the biggest bears on Earth.

These huge **predators** are very strong and have 42 sharp teeth.

paw

Polar bears have thick fur that looks white and keeps them warm.

They even have furry paws that help them walk on ice and snow.

Where do polar bears live?

Arctic

Polar bears live in the **Arctic**.

In the Arctic it is light all day and all night for part of the summer.

In the Arctic it is dark all day and all night for part of the winter.

This **polar** area is one of the coldest places on Earth!

What do polar bears do in the day?

In midsummer, polar bears are most **active** in the morning and early afternoon.

They wake up after sleeping on ice or in snow **pits**.

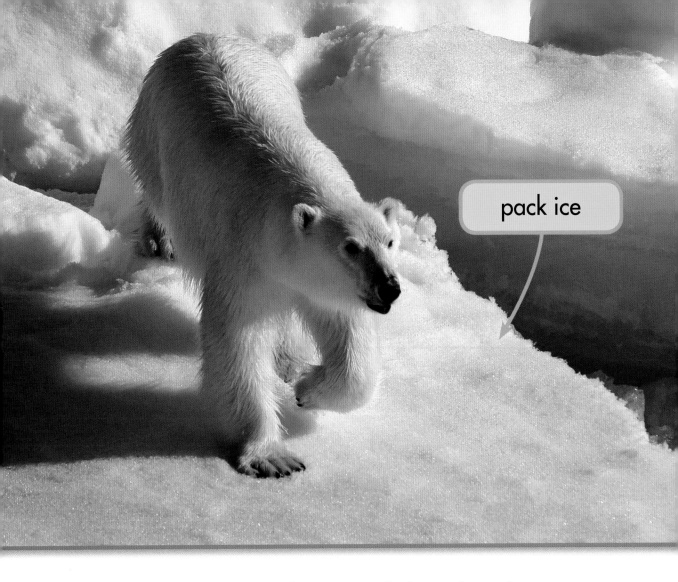

pack ice

Polar bears spend part of the day hunting for food.

They catch a lot of their food around moving ice called pack ice.

What do polar bears eat?

seal

Polar bears use their strong sense of smell to hunt seals.

They also eat dead whales and walruses that wash up near the shore.

Polar bears will feed on almost anything.

This includes everything from reindeer and birds, to berries and rubbish!

What threatens polar bears?

Polar bears are the top **Arctic predators**, so most animals do not threaten them.

Killer whales and humans are their main enemies.

Pollution is a serious threat to polar bears, because it causes rising temperatures.

This leads to melting ice which endangers the food and homes of polar bears.

Do polar bears live in groups?

Polar bears do not usually live in groups.

These **mammals** spend much of their time alone.

Sometimes a small group of polar bears feed together in the same area.

Mother polar bears also live with their babies for one to three years.

What do polar bears do at night?

Polar bears spend quite a lot of time resting, both in the day and at night.

In midsummer, polar bears often sleep or rest near the end of the day.

Polar bears sleep for about seven or eight hours, similar to humans.

Many curl up and nap in snow **pits** or on blocks of ice.

What are baby polar bears like?

Baby polar bears are called cubs.

A mother polar bear usually gives birth to two cubs at a time.

The helpless babies grow bigger as they drink their mother's milk.

The cubs learn how to hunt and survive on their own in just 18 to 30 months!

Polar bear body map

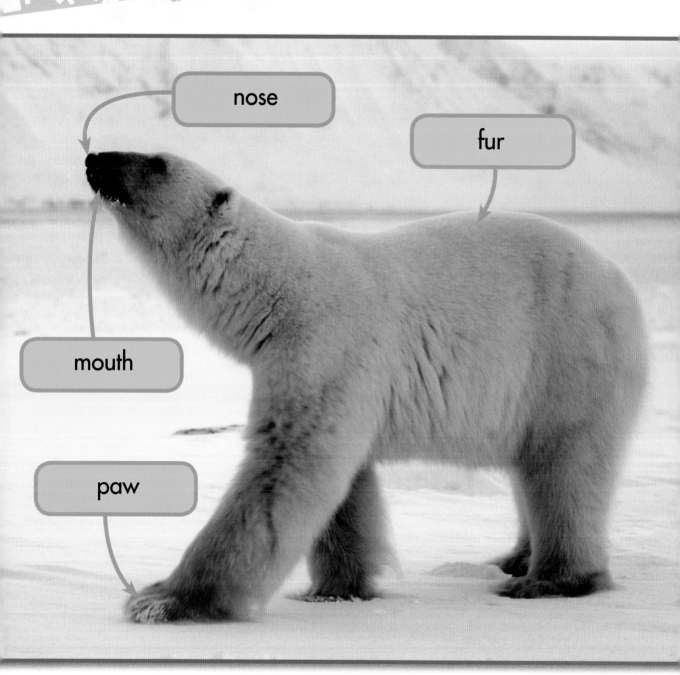

nose

fur

mouth

paw

Glossary

active busy doing lots of things

Arctic area surrounding the North Pole. It is very cold in the Arctic.

mammal animal that feeds its babies milk. All mammals have some hair or fur on their bodies.

pit large hole

polar extremely cold areas at the top and bottom of the world

pollution harmful dirt, waste gases or chemicals, that damage the environment

predator animal that hunts and kills other animals for food

Find out more

Books

Arctic and Antarctic (Eye Wonder), Lorie Mack (DK Publishing, 2006)
Where Do Polar Bears Live?, Sarah Thomson. (Collins, 2010).

Websites

www.kidzone.ws/sg/polarbear/polar_bear.htm
Learn about where polar bears live and find out all about them on this website.

www.kids.nationalgeographic.com/kids/animals/creaturefeature/polar-bear/
Watch a video on polar bears and discover polar bear facts on the National Geographic website.

Index